AFTER
WINTER,
SPRING

AFTER WINTER, SPRING

by

Nita Schuh

LOGOS INTERNATIONAL
Plainfield, New Jersey

All Scripture references are taken from
the Revised Standard Version of the Holy Bible,
except where noted as KJV (King James Version).

AFTER WINTER, SPRING
Copyright © 1978 by Logos International
All rights reserved
Printed in the United States of America
Library of Congress Catalog Card Number: 78-64345
International Standard Book Number: 0-88270-284-X
Logos International, Plainfield, New Jersey 07060

For Joe

Acknowledgments

Excerpt from *Collected Poems* of Miss Edna St. Vincent Millay, Harper & Row. Copyright 1917, 1945 by Edna St. Vincent Millay. Used with permission.

Excerpts from *A Grief Observed* by C.S. Lewis. Copyright © 1961 by N.W. Clerk. Used by permission of The Seabury Press, Inc.

Excerpt from "Jones Beach," from *Never a Greater Need,* by Walter Benton. Published Feb. 9, 1948, Reprinted six times. Eighth printing, January 1957. Published by Alfred A. Knopf, Inc., New York. Used by permission.

Excerpt from "At a Window" in *The Complete Poems of Carl Sandburg.* Copyright, 1916, by Holt, Rinehart and Winston, Inc.; copyright, 1944, by Carl Sandburg. Reprinted by permission of Harcourt Brace Jovanovich, Inc.

Excerpt from *The Complete Poems of Emily Dickinson,* edited by Thomas H. Johnson. Used by permission of Little, Brown and Company.

Excerpt from "A Leaf-Treader," from *The Poetry of Robert Frost,* edited by Edward Connery Lathem. Word copyright © 1936 by Robert Frost. Word copyright © 1964 by Lesley Frost Ballantine. Word copyright © 1969 by Holt, Rinehart and Winston, Inc. Reprinted by permission of Holt, Rinehart and Winston, publishers.

And after winter, followeth green may.

"Troilus and Criseyde"
Geoffrey Chaucer

Foreword

This is a very personal account of a very private grief—my own following the death of my husband.

I do not believe one can know in advance how one will grieve. It is likewise impossible to know how prolonged the grief process will be, or by what means recovery eventually may be achieved. For some, it seems to happen quickly. I use the word "seems" because it is impossible to know exactly what another person is feeling or experiencing. Others require a longer period in which to come to terms with the death of someone very important in their lives. I belong to this second category.

I endured many of the emotions familiar to the bereaved: shock, disbelief, sleeplessness, loss of appetite. I fantasized about my own early death that would quickly reunite me with my beloved.

Almost immediately—perhaps too soon—I returned to a demanding job where I went through the motions of living almost normally. But it was a charade; soon I knew that this game playing was fair to neither my employers nor myself.

I resigned my position, redecorated my house, and traveled. I read prodigiously, literally losing myself in books. Always a lover of literature, I now haunted the libraries, reading for many hours every day, substituting the words of others for those I would like to have spoken or written—words that somehow would convey the pain I felt and the awful struggle that threatened my very survival. I also hoped to find revealed somewhere in all those words a formula by which others had discovered peace and comfort. Since it appeared that the Lord had other plans than a quick demise for me, I somehow had to emerge from this conflict alive—really alive and whole again.

Months passed. Summer gave way to autumn, normally my favorite season of the year. But now nothing seemed worthwhile. Inertia had replaced my former vivacity, depriving me of the initiative scarcely to *be*, much less *do*. Loneliness, despondency, feelings of inadequacy—these, and the monumental effort to conceal from observant family and friends how I really felt, sapped all my vitality. I realized I was much too introspective; but the truth is, I didn't care about anything at all except how miserable I was and how much I missed Joe.

Companion to all this, and adding to my unutterable sadness, was an overwhelming sense of guilt—a terrible conviction of failure to demonstrate almost any Christian virtue. Previously, I had felt I was endowed with at least a few such qualities. I had been a Christian since childhood; at other times in my life when problems or adversity had struck, I had been able to turn to God for guidance and comfort. Now it seemed the faith I had so long professed, and by which my husband had both lived and died, had deserted me. I searched everywhere—almost frantically—for God; but the more resolutely I looked for Him, the more His presence eluded me. Desolation engulfed me.

"You'll be okay, Nita! You have such courage, such faith! And you're so strong! You'll be just fine," people said. In fact, it was said so often, and so confidently, I must have projected to others that I, indeed, possessed these qualities of strength and character. But they were wrong. I had little of these, and I wasn't fine. Not at all.

I tried—really tried—to rededicate my life (whatever remained of it) to God. I hoped it would be mercifully brief. I prayed to feel His presence. But more often than not, the presence I found myself longing for most of all was that of my husband, without whom I felt incomplete, empty, separated from all that made me feel whole, worthy, loved.

What one does, finally, to mitigate grief and how one comes to terms with death's reality and finality are as individualistic as the persons involved. My personal belief is that, for professing Christians, it helps to study the Bible; to read testimonies of faith and hope; and, above all, to pray—even when (perhaps *especially* when) one loses the capacity to pray, as I often did. This condition is described by Elizabeth Barrett Browning as being like having a wandering mind that is too near to God to pray at all. Beyond these, I believe one should do, within reasonable limits, what seems to offer the most comfort and hope.

For me, to whom words always have had an almost magical quality—who always has had a need to verbalize everything—writing seemed to offer a way out of my personal extremity.

It came about almost accidentally. Sometime during the early months of my widowhood I began to end many days by sitting down at my desk and typing my thoughts and feelings. At first, usually without giving them a second glance, I tore them up and tossed the pieces into a wastebasket. But writing about Joe and our love—my need for him—helped make me feel less alone; it evoked his presence in a way that made the house less of a solitary cell for me. Cruel and senseless though I knew the delusion to be, it became something of a "game of pretend" that he was only "away"—as he had often been during the navy years when I had ended every day with a letter or taped message to him.

Soon I was writing each day *for myself alone.* I was including as nearly as possible what I had been thinking or feeling that day, what I was *being* at that moment. It was a diary of what I could not say or admit to anyone and scarcely dared think. Thus began a sort of daily exercise when, without shame or pretense, I could, for those few moments, be *myself*—weak, sad, lonely, angry—whatever. And though I no longer destroyed what I wrote, neither did anyone know of the practice. I hoped that it would help me achieve not only a passive acceptance of what I could not change but that I also might rediscover a *raison d'être* and some direction for whatever remained of my life.

Naturally there was much repetition as, day after day, I experienced many of the same emotions, and was assailed by the same doubts, fears, frustrations, longings, and needs. Nevertheless, I faithfully recorded what was uppermost in my mind and thoughts—what had impressed me most, memories that both helped and haunted. I think I also wrote to reassure myself in some oblique, imprecise way, that sometime mourning would be behind me—that I'd no longer have such a need to articulate a grief that was unlike anything I had ever experienced before and left me questioning my identity, my womanhood.

The question arises: If, as I have stated, I wrote solely for myself, why now expose those writings to public view?

In a conversation with a widowed friend, I remarked, "Sometimes I have difficulty remembering anything good or right I ever did in my marriage. Though most of the time I know this isn't true, I sometimes feel I was a total failure in making Joe happy."

"Oh, I'm *so* glad you said that," she exclaimed. "I thought I was the only one who ever felt that way, so I never told anyone. I didn't dare say it for fear people would not understand." She added, "My husband died three years ago and I occasionally still have those awful moments of wondering what I did right!"

Other people *did* share some of the doubts, feelings of

inadequacy that I felt. And my friend, at least, had been relieved that another person was willing to say so.

Too, the more I searched what many gifted writers had to say, the more I realized nearly everything I read was written "after the fact," that is, after grief had been overcome; after closed doors had opened onto brighter vistas; after faith, reborn, had revitalized the person and brought renewed peace and happiness. I found almost nothing that had been written during the actual time of one's greatest battles and defeats; I could find only little that had been written before healing had taken place and wholeness had been restored.

While I had felt consolation from some of these writings, none revealed the inexpressible loneliness, alienation and even self-pity, when, having lost all that mattered to me, I was desperately trying to recover enough courage to hang on for just one more day.

Was it possible, I asked myself, that my intimate outpourings of grief might help others similarly stricken? It is in that hope that these reflections—representative excerpts of a year's diary—are offered. Authentic, unretouched, they are a self-portrait of my grief.

AFTER WINTER, SPRING

Wednesday, January 1

Immutably, on schedule, the new year begins, notwithstanding my illogical wish to postpone or avert it altogether. How different it is from every other New Year's Day! And how I have hated the thought of beginning a new year without my beloved Joe! As long as I was able to say, "My husband died *this* year," it somehow seemed I did not quite have to acknowledge that our shining hour has passed. I cannot cope with that thought; not yet, anyway.

I feel so alone! Nothing but emptiness surrounds, engulfs me! It is as though all that is left of me is a caricature wearing my clothes, masquerading as me. All of the important things that ever could happen already have happened; there is no present, only the past which blots out all other time frames. The real *me*—the *me* I was with and through Joe—died when he died. Absent now is the person I had become because of his love and whom I knew and rather liked. I miss *me*, and oh, I miss *him*, the relationship that was *us*, and all that was familiar and loved.

And yet, from somewhere deep inside me, on this day of resolutions and new beginnings, I know I must look ahead, not back; must learn, somehow, to live creatively again. If not, I invalidate everything our love was and all that we were and had during that lovely summery interlude that is now history. I cannot return to that irreplaceable yesterday alone. In some way, I must find meaning where none exists; I must respond to an inaudible call to arise, to get on with the business of living, however diminished, changed, and barren life now seems.

It is, indeed, a new year.

Friday, January 3

My first thought upon awakening this morning was, "Today, a year ago, we flew to Hawaii." What happy days those were; yet they were strangely filled with foreboding. Somehow I knew that was not only our today; it also was our tomorrow. Our forever was running out like the final grains of sand in an hourglass, ineluctably and swiftly.

I lay in bed and pondered: Just how much did Joe feel, *know* this to be true? There were moments when he held me close and said, "Oh, darling, all I have really ever wanted has been for you to be happy." At such moments I was certain he was telling me that he did know, and he was trying to help me face that fact. Still, he never seemed to wish to pursue the subject—he didn't dwell upon it. Instead, he constantly was planning yet another adventure for the future. Was this his way of dealing with an inescapable fact he knew he could not change? However hard one tries, one cannot fully enter into the mind of another, can never fully share another's fear or pain. And Joe was not one to verbalize worries.

One awful night on Maui, when he was too exhausted to eat or to even undress, I sleeplessly listened all night for his breathing, wondering if he would be alive in the morning. So many memories! As thankful as I am for the countless happy ones, right now it is the other kind that seem in control. How effortlessly I surrender to these sad, negative thoughts, and how I detest myself for doing so! Still, when one has neither love nor hope, it is difficult to be optimistic or, for that matter, to manifest other virtues of character. I seem to be in very short supply of any such redeeming qualities.

When our dog, Happy, and I went for our walk around nine o'clock, the stars were out for the first time in ages.

Quickly I looked for "my star to wish upon," the one I look for each night and think it somehow is a beacon of communication between Joe and me. I don't remember exactly when I first felt this—soon after his death, I think. But he seems nearer, in a strange, indefinable way, as I walk under the stars with Happy, the way we used to do.

It is no accident, I believe, that, throughout the ages, sojourners—on whatever road, to whatever des-tination—have been guided by these heavenly torchlights. Remote, compelling in their ordered galaxies, they have given direction out of all sorts of lost conditions.

As I walk under a Texas sky, dark but for a myriad of stars this night, I pray that I, too, may find my way; may be guided toward a future that, at the moment, seems as dark and unfathomable as all the mysteries of the universe.

Monday, January 6

Today, Joe's birthday, has been spent remembering him and some of the ways in which we celebrated birthdays—his and mine. Try as I would, I never could plan as ingeniously, or surprise him in quite the way he often did me; and I've remembered some of the things I loved and admired most about him.

Some of the qualities he had in greater abundance than most of us were courage, optimism, creativity, and a delightful sense of humor. He had tremendous faith; but one thing that set him apart from others was his unfailing kindness—always—to everyone. He simply could not be pressured, provoked, or rushed into unkindness. And he was very thoughtful, especially of older persons and those less fortunate than ourselves. The kinds of things most people rarely do, even with effort, he did easily, or so it seemed.

He also had an enormous capacity for caring and *really cared* about more people and things—and all animals!—than anyone else I've ever known.

As for me, he made me more than I ever could have been without him. Unselfishly, he spotlighted my good qualities and overlooked the many lesser ones. All the things I otherwise never should have become, I was because he understood me, believed in me, encouraged me. And, most of all, loved me.

Tuesday, January 7

Our perennial January "false spring" has arrived in Texas. Today the temperature was in the upper seventies and it actually seemed hot. The first year we lived here, we cleaned the goldfish pond during Christmas week, wading in with our bare feet. After all those years in cold climates, we hardly could believe our December weather and Joe asked, "Who needs a palm tree when we can get a sunburn watching the Cotton Bowl game on New Year's Day?" We had endured cold weather for many years and it was such a luxury to us to enjoy spring-like weather in the wintertime.

I took down the Christmas tree and put away the crèche and other holiday decorations.

For a long time we wanted a crèche. When we attended the Passion Play in Oberammergau we saw many beautifully carved figures and longed for some of them. Most, however, were too expensive for us. Each year, when Christmas approached, Joe would again express a longing for a really artistic crèche.

Last year, a few weeks before the holidays, he saw one at the Gift Market that he liked very much. I urged him to purchase it as an early "us" present. How carefully he uncrated those precious figures and arranged them to create the nativity scene. Did he consider, as he untrimmed the tree and stored the crèche after Christmas, that he would not do so again? I tried to imagine what it would be like, but concluded I am glad God does not fully reveal these things to us. The knowledge would be too awesome for most of us, certainly for me.

I thought of a quote I have either read or heard: "Acceptance is the first law of the wounded spirit." Joe seemed to understand this and to live by it; I haven't reached that point. No doubt this accounts, in part, for his serenity and its near absence from my life.

Sunday, January 12

It is Super Bowl Sunday, and for a fleeting moment I thought how wonderful it would be if I could open the door, walk into the library, and find Joe in his favorite chair, watching the game. I wanted it *so much* that, irresistibly, I was drawn to the scene and was left feeling devastated when I discovered his chair was empty. Only one who has experienced a similar thing can understand this irrational act, I suppose. Needless to say, I no longer cared who won the game, and I could not watch it.

Over and over today, I've found myself thinking about heaven as a literal, definable place, and wondering what it is like there—what celestial things occupy Joe this day. I cannot guess why, on this particular Sunday, such thoughts should dominate my consciousness. But they do. I try to put it in the context of The Revelation and it is easy for me to imagine the hosts of heaven praising and adoring God; but what else happens there?

Happy is like a frisky puppy as we take our late evening walk in the crisp night air. The stars are shining brightly, cupped in a cold and clear sky. They seem very close and luminous. I feel Joe's presence as I have not felt it throughout the day—but as I often do under a starry sky. Is this because it is almost impossible to observe this familiar, yet always breath-taking phenomenon without feeling a oneness with the universe and with God?

I search the sky: for God or for Joe? It doesn't matter, for here, in the star-strewn night, I find them both, if only for a moment. Past, present and future merge into a timeless eternity in which there is no yesterday, today, tomorrow. Only forever in a heaven that, however real I believe it to be, just now seems evanescent and very remote.

7

Tuesday, January 14

I have been invited to visit friends in Virginia and, as I prepare for the journey, I find myself going about the house looking intently at some of my favorite things. They, of course, are mere material possessions and I view them as such. At times in my life I have owned almost nothing of material value, and I know I could manage without many material things again, should that be called for. Yet many of these items have great meaning to me because of the circumstances under which they were acquired, their association with Joe, or, more probably, because they were gifts from him. I wonder as I do this if he, too, ever took such an inventory—especially when reason tells me he knew he was about to take the ultimate journey from which there is no return.

Not that I have such thoughts about myself; that is not what prompted this little survey. Or is it? Any time one goes on a trip there is the possibility that he may not return. And death is never far from my thoughts these days. Not my own, necessarily; just *death.*

The degree to which I have been preoccupied with the subject must have been reflected in the way I've pressed my attorney to revise my will, to make certain that all of my business affairs are in order, and to be sure he understands all of my "final" instructions! And those letters of assurance I've written to my family! In all these, I am declaring that death, should it come to me in the near future, will not find me unready and unwelcoming!

As I continue my household cataloguing, my heart is filled with gratitude to God, to Joe, and to mama and dad (who loaned us the down payment) for the joy we shared in this house. After a navy career that required many geographical relocations, this was the house that became home to me as no other except that of my childhood.

What I'm discovering, I think, is that I'd rather be here than anywhere else. It is even better than being with loved friends whose home has welcomed me for many years. I know I'll enjoy seeing them, once I am there. And I am deeply grateful for their love and for the fact they want me to visit them. Still, this night I am glad not only for the physical shelter of this house—I also am glad for the familiarity and dearness of surroundings that speak home and security and love in a very comforting way. I hope I never have to move again—ever.

Capsule impressions from the preceding ten days:

Trying to imagine Joe on the seat beside me on the flight into Dulles International Airport—alas, the heart would not ratify this wish. He wasn't there. Years ago, when a plane had taken him from me, he had written:

"I'd like to throw rocks at this empty seat beside me. Remembering how wonderful it is to have you near, to hold your hand, to anticipate arrival, to share a glass of wine, and to have you fall asleep with your head on my shoulder—these are some of the things that make this trip so disappointingly different from those we have taken together. . . ." My sentiments exactly, darling!

A beautiful, soft, feathery snowfall, continuing all day, covered everything with a shimmery whiteness. This scene re-created in my memory a snow-covered hill at the Nellie Custis mansion when, like gleeful children who believed in the saying, "And they lived happily ever after," Joe and I had tobogganed on a Sunday afternoon years ago.

The hauntingly beautiful songs of her love and longing for Odysseus and her need for his presence that Penelope sang in a performance of *Odyssey* at the John F. Kennedy Center for the Performing Arts—how well I understood her despair and loneliness! While Odysseus traveled from place to place for so many years, beautiful Penelope waited and longed for him with many tears. I easily identified with them both—the Penelope of ancient Greece and the contemporary one of the play. There is so little new to women who have lost love.

The absolutely astounding and breath-taking Chinese archaeological exhibit at the National Gallery of Art—a once-in-a-lifetime experience! The artifacts, some dating back six hundred thousand years, create a profoundly moving and unforgettable exhibit, the most exciting I have seen since the Louvre! The most exquisite piece was *The Flying Horse*, a bronze sculpture that ranks, in my estimation, with the *Pieta* and *David* in artistic perfection and beauty. And, oh, Joe! How I longed to share this rare event with you, who taught me so much—all I know, really—about all art forms. I tried to view it through your appreciative and art-loving eyes.

My friends, who love me, say, "You must make a new life." They do not fully comprehend that this is precisely what I am forced to do—daily—no matter how distasteful and repugnant it is to me. A widowed acquaintance says only, "Here is a book that helped me. I think it also might help you." It has and does. Thank you.

The shared glances, the little intimacies of the longtime married, the unconscious gesture, the "oneness" so evident in my beloved friends—all of these reminded me that these were also mine. And in the spirit of love and caring that had prompted them to urge me to make another life, I wanted to say to them, "You are so lucky! Don't waste a precious moment of this togetherness; enjoy, enjoy! However long love lasts, it is never long enough!"

The return flight—the desire to be home again, to see Happy, to find Joe, whose presence I could not feel in the familiar, yet now strange, beauty of Virginia. In my friends' hospitable home—though I was surrounded by their love—I felt isolated and very, very lonely, as though I were playing an unaccustomed and unrehearsed role for which I had no aptitude. There was a need—no, *an urgency*—to hurry home to Joe's memory. The way it used to be when I'd want to hurry home with him, and to bed, to be loved to sleep.

Wednesday, January 29

A cold, gloomy morning fits my mood perfectly. I spend most of the day by the fire in the library, ostensibly reading. But I cannot concentrate and so I find it easier to watch the flames and think of nothing, my mind as inert and vacuous as my body is listless. It would be easy to go through the remainder of my life just like this, seeing no one, doing nothing, blanking out all thought. I almost prefer these feelings of emptiness and nothingness to the even greater pain and terror of the challenge of making decisions, of being confronted with reality.

Paradoxically, I almost hate the fact that I now have so much leisure time when I had so little during Joe's lifetime. Before, there never was enough time; now there is too much. I feel guilty and grief-stricken that I need not rush to get my work done when then I *always* had to hurry, hurry, hurry to barely stay even. Oh, how I wish I hadn't been so harried, rushed, frantic, and exhausted in those days. What compulsion there was within me to get everything done, as though in the doing I could dispel worry, could substitute activity for anxiety. Now nothing seems worth the doing.

And yes, I was scared—so very, very terrified! I didn't *want* to live in a constant state of fear that he would die, but I did. It was as though I were engaged in a never-ending tug of war with God for Joe—yet somehow knowing all the while what the ultimate outcome would be. For from the outset it was a no-win struggle for me. I kept losing, inexorably, inch by painful inch. Yet I could not give in, could not let go of my grip, or all would be irretrievably lost. There are many who would fault me—would say I *should* have been able to relinquish Joe, to say to God, "Thy will be done." Well, I couldn't—not then, anyway.

But I did try—earnestly try—to overcome my unreasoning and debilitating fear which imprisoned me for all those last twenty-six months of his life. It was such a monstrous, unwelcome companion, casting a great, black shadow night and day, haunting me. How Joe must have hated that, he who overcame fear (for surely he knew it now and then) and lived so victoriously.

Please, God, may he have understood what caused this awful fear—how it was for me to contemplate life without him—and never hated *me* for it.

Perhaps the fact that one person was that important and meant that much to me should have been as frightening as the prospect of losing him. But I never thought of that. And, in truth, I guess I didn't think of much of anything but how *I* needed him! It is painful to admit, but I realize now I didn't even give that much thought to how Joe felt about it. I suppose I assumed he needed me in the same way.

We both needed God more than we needed each other. Joe knew this a long, long time before I did and accepted it with equanimity, even while I still fought the idea.

Oh, dear Lord, forgive me for failing to trust you—for failing to attain the perfect love for you that, according to your Word, casts out fear.

Even though I do not deserve your love, help me through this uncertain night, this new year when my mind and heart cry that they cannot accept the end of all that seemed meaningful and beautiful in my life.

Saturday, February 1

A new month—how slowly the days pass, one into another, with little more to mark their passage than turning the page on the calendar.

It rained very hard last night and continued throughout the day. I decided to reread portions of Joe's letters to me and spent the day before the fire, reading and remembering. I have read only a limited number of the total but they make me feel very loved—the first time I've felt this alive since he died.

The mere rereading of his beautiful words of love gives me a very warm glow. Should I spend so much time reliving the past? Probably not. My mind tells me I must get on with living now—today—choosing neither the past, which is over, nor the future which may or may not appear. Nevertheless, reading these letters is extremely therapeutic just now and very, very reassuring. They are the nearest thing to something warm and human and responsive that I can evoke. Oh, I was truly loved! And that knowledge and reminder revalidate me to myself. How I have needed that!

Why is it that widowhood has so robbed me of self-esteem, and masked my sense of value as a person? Not as a child of God, about which, paradoxically, I feel secure; but as a worthwhile member of the human family, about which I previously had few doubts.

The rains continued and I read far into the night. Happy deserted me, looking reproachfully at me when I wouldn't give up and come on into the bedroom at our usual bedtime. I remained beside the burned-out fire, communing with my lost love and remembering. And, oh, it was beautiful! Memories, someone has said, have magical ways of bringing back nice yesterdays. There are so many that I recall with gratitude this lonely night.

Not all of my memories are happy ones, of course, but the letters express his love very passionately and beautifully. Many have made me laugh—the first time in ages. Joe enjoyed my laughter and said he would rather hear me "bubble" than anyone, referring to my exuberant whoops as a "symphony of happy sounds." Oh, darling, did I forget how to laugh during those last months when crisis collided with crisis? Dear God, I did, I did! I tried to recall when I last *really* laughed and am saddened to realize I cannot remember! Oh, my darling, forgive me for depriving you of this joy! I wasn't even aware it was happening; it is only now that I realize how terribly true it is that I seem to have forgotten laughter.

As I put away the letters for the night I thought of a play we saw in London some years ago. Called *Dear Love,* it was the love story of Robert and Elizabeth Barrett Browning. When they were secretly planning to be wed and to sail for Italy, Robert suggested to Elizabeth that she pack very sparingly because they would have to pay dearly for every ounce. Because she could not bear to part with a single letter, Elizabeth ignored this advice, taking all of his notes to her. Years later, just prior to her death, she found great comfort and joy in once again reading them.

I understand this and am grateful that, despite the many moves we made and the often limited space, I, too, kept all of my love letters from Joe. Like Mrs. Browning, I am comforted and once again feel feminine and loved and warmed on this rainy, cold, first-of-February night.

Sunday, February 2

Happy got a quick morning walk. It was one of those times I wished I could have opened the back door and said to him, "There's a great big yard, all for you!" But, as usual, he would have none of it and looked at me as if to question, "What in the world is the matter with you this morning?"

The matter was that I wanted to rush back to my letters. I wanted to get up, make a quick pot of coffee, retrieve the morning paper, brush my teeth and climb back into bed with Joe for a leisurely time of coffee-flavored kisses, the Sunday papers and a day off from everything but being loved, needed, wanted.

I wanted to re-create—even in fantasy—a sense of Joe's nearness and of my own contentment from lying in bed beside him.

But Happy understood none of this. Nor would the vast majority of people, I suppose. Nevertheless, this realization did not deter me and I spent another day responding in my own way to words of love written over a dozen-year span that now seemed more important than any future years that may be yet to be lived.

Thursday, February 6

Two absurdly traumatic experiences dominated my day. In the afternoon I purchased some lingerie, the first I have bought for myself since becoming Joe's wife. He liked very feminine and beautiful lingerie and enjoyed giving me these exquisite gifts, thereby keeping me well supplied with pretty "unmentionables" all the years. The realization that not only would he never again give me such beautiful and intimate things but, more importantly, he also would never again admire me in them, nullified in one brief moment all feelings of femininity, of being loved, protected, and desired.

In the evening, I entertained old friends at dinner. Without thinking, I sat down at my accustomed place at the dining table which had *not* been set for service, instead of the host's place—Joe's place—which *had* been set for me! Such a silly thing to have become upset about; but it unnerved me utterly. And I fought tears all during dinner to my own discomfiture and that of my guests.

Just when I think I am making progress the fragile threads of control break in a thousand pieces. And in an exaggerated sense of feeling sorry for myself I think, "It was kinder when the widow was placed on the funeral pyre and consumed along with her husband's body."

Friday, February 14

Valentine's Day—another "first" without my beloved—a day for lovers, for couples, a day to hold hands and whisper sweet nothings. In short, a day that shouldn't be in the calendar of those who walk alone. I looked long at the beautiful, old-fashioned Valentine that hangs, framed, on my bedroom wall and I reflected on Valentine's Days in the past when Joe always gave me something romantic, sentimental, and beautiful. And usually a silly Valentine card too!

I listened to the love poems he recorded for a Valentine gift once upon a happier time; and I remembered the year we presented each other identical albums of love songs.

I remembered a time during our courtship when he found a Valentine card of two beautiful monarch butterflies. It read, "Butterflies count the moments, not the months," and he gave this to me along with a silk "Vera" blouse, hand painted with the same beautiful monarch butterflies! It was a reminder that I should be grateful for the many happy moments we were privileged to share, a reminder I need very much to heed once again.

So, as you might wish, darling, I am concentrating on the many beautiful moments—fleeting and gossamer though they were—and I *am* grateful to have been loved by you. I am deeply thankful for Valentine's Days remembered, and for all of the "days in the sun" that were ours. I was, after all, one of the lucky ones! I shall try harder to remember that.

Tuesday, February 18

Today there was a telephone call from a longtime friend. He and Joe had served in the navy together and had shared many career experiences out of which grew a strong bond of friendship that lasted through the years. But, as often happens with those we've known in military service, we had pretty much lost contact and had not communicated with him for some time.

After the usual preliminaries and inquiring about me, he said, "Let me speak to that no-good husband of yours."

Abruptly—almost too quickly—I told him, "Joe is dead!"

After a moment of stunned silence he blurted out, "You're kidding!" He knew, of course, I couldn't have made that statement in jest. When he did grasp the fact that Joe was, indeed, dead, he tried to apologize for having referred to him as my "no-good" husband, and then, to my astonishment, he began to cry with harsh, rasping sobs.

Struggling for control he finally said, "It seems I cannot remember a time when Joe and I were not friends. I didn't really think about it, I just always expected him to be there—even though we saw and heard from one another infrequently. I feel so much poorer for his death."

As do we all, my dear friend. Thank you for saying so. I'm glad you cared enough to miss Joe—and to weep.

Sunday, February 23

Around midnight last night it began to snow and, unusual though it is for this part of Texas, it continued throughout the night. Happy and I were out on our walk very early, around 6:30 A.M.—in the untrammeled, pristine whiteness before anyone else was about.

All was quiet softness; an ethereal beauty surrounded us and in the silence we walked. I felt closer to God than I had felt for a long time. I wished for the gifts of an artist or a poet, the better to express the momentary harmony I felt within and my sense of wonder at His world about me.

Happy, too, enjoyed the unfamiliar snow, running with gay abandon as though he were a young puppy trying to figure out what had happened to his accustomed landmarks. For that moment, each of us was captured by our extraordinary surroundings and each, in keeping with his particular nature and inclination said, "Hello, world, you're beautiful!"

Before noon the clouds disappeared. The sun came out in a bright blue sky, and by mid-afternoon, the snow was gone except in a few shaded areas. So much beauty, but so short-lived—the way it always seems to be with all things beautiful. But for those short hours I *almost* felt alive again; I almost felt a godly "yes" erasing all of the negatives of the recent past. It was a lovely interlude—so unexpected and like a benefaction.

Friday, February 28

Awake early, Happy and I were on our way to visit dad, driving in the rain that continues to fall. The drive was lovely despite the downpour, and there are signs of spring everywhere—due, no doubt, to the warm days we had in January and the early rains that have fallen for nearly a week now.

There is a light, misty, almost transparent, pale green haze surrounding the trees as if God had touched them overnight with a celestial paintbrush dipped in the palest emerald hues. If one concentrates on a single tree, the color is hardly visible at all; in groupings, it definitely is there, a faint hint of more to come.

Strangely, from a distance it looks almost golden; then, as one approaches nearer, the greens become more vivid, a marked contrast to the red oaks whose brown leaves still cling—a reminder that winter has, after all, not entirely passed, however much the young spring greenings promise.

In the pastures I saw lots of new calves snuggling close to their mothers and I cried, "Look, Happy, at the big puppies," unconsciously employing the funny, endearing expression Joe had coined in pointing out the cattle to Happy who would nearly jump out of the car looking for them on our drives to the country in times past.

And the daffodils—undulating blankets of golden yellow, a sight to fill one's senses with sunshine and renewed faith.

Thank you, God, for greening of trees, new calves, bright yellow blossoms; for your age-old, ever-new promise that spring will come again—and again. Thank you, however much I have doubted it this winter of my soul's lament.

Monday, March 3

I've begun to cry too much of late and I must try harder to get this under control. I think maybe it is because of the quick succession of so many sad anniversaries, the remembrance of which dominates my thoughts. But the steady flow of tears is making a wreck of me; and poor Happy, who quite naturally doesn't understand what the matter is, is extremely upset and disturbed over this doleful state of affairs.

One of the problems is that the dreams—nightmares, really—continue, in which Joe always is having another heart attack and is desperately ill. I try to get help, carrying him up endless flights of stairs, down dark, dark corridors—never, never arriving at our destination. I awaken traumatized, crying, and drained. Seldom can I get back to sleep, whatever the hour at which I am awake. Oh, how I long for these evil dreams to cease. Of course, I would welcome dreaming pleasantly of Joe and of our relationship. That would be a real joy; so far, such dreams have eluded me.

For days I've been trying to follow the scriptural admonition to "give thanks in all circumstances; for this is the will of God in Christ Jesus for you" (1 Thess. 5:18). That is pretty literal: *in all circumstances!* But does it mean, as some maintain, that we are to thank God for *everything* that happens to us, regardless of how petty or terrible? Or, as I believe, does it mean *despite* the circumstances in which we may find ourselves, God still loves us and cares about us and we, therefore, should give thanks for that love and care? If the latter, this makes sense to me, and I think I can usually follow it without too much difficulty. But if the former, well, that doesn't make sense to me. I don't believe God wants His children to suffer and I really doubt He wants us to thank Him for faulty plumbing and other such trivial problems.

Through all of life's vicissitudes, though, He does love us and we are to praise Him. About this I have no doubts.

Friday, March 7

The redbud trees are in bloom, reminding me of the difficulty we encountered in finally getting two of them to grow in the yard. We didn't know much about gardening in Texas and we had to replace those trees time and time again before we got any to take root. Redbud—a singular name for a tree that produces purple-pink blossoms: these trees are lovely and their early blossoming is a sure sign of spring's advent throughout much of the southland.

On my walk this afternoon with Happy I found some pear blossoms that had been trimmed from trees and left in an alleyway. I brought them home and arranged them in Joe's grandmother's cut crystal vase and they are beautiful. There is a distinctive, fresh fragrance about them that I remember from childhood—evoking memories of the old pear tree in the garden at home. Dad says that tree has blossomed and produced fruit for over sixty years.

My first year away from home in college, barely sixteen years old, I was so homesick! Strangely, one of the things I missed was that old pear tree. On my first visit home, I ran into the garden and jumped up and touched one of the lower limbs of that tree, evidently reassuring myself that it, and all it represented, was still intact! Extraordinary that the sight and scent of these pear blossoms should evoke such long-buried memories! I was giddy with happiness to be home with mama and dad and to see everything that was familiar. And to feel secure and loved.

Oh, I wish, like that sixteen-year-old kid, I could feel that loved and secure again!

Tuesday, March 11

It rained the day my darling died
And each day since . . .
If not from the heavens,
In my heart.

+ + +

I saw a rainbow in the sky today
And remembered God's everlasting covenant
Between himself, Noah, and future generations
Never to again destroy the world with water.

Did the rainbow I viewed on high
Also hold a promise to me—His assurance
That my tears will not always flow;
That my world, destroyed by your death,
Will live again?
Is such a miracle possible?

For miracles
And everlasting covenants,
Both old and new,
Thank you, God.

Saturday, March 15

This has been a brilliant, sunshiny day followed by a night of equal splendor as a full moon gently soars through a star-spangled sky. No ides of March portent dares intrude upon the peace and serenity of this—God's world—the magnificence of which is impressed upon one's consciousness at every turn.

The sun's warm rays touch the earth with soft caresses, the almost immediate reward for which is tender, new growth everywhere. The panorama of nature becomes more predominantly green; but not entirely so as blossoming tulip trees, japonica bushes, early flowering hawthorn and daffodils—among others—vie for their fair share of attention and admiration.

The longest nights of the year are over; days are lengthening. One is almost persuaded that winter soon will be past and spring, that elusive beauty which flirts about in seventy-five-degree temperature one day, coyly disappears behind a Texas norther the next, only to reappear more dazzling and seductive on the morrow, will be here to stay.

For lo, the winter is past,
the rain is over and gone.
The flowers appear on the earth,
the time of singing has come.
(Song of Sol. 2:11-12)

And after winter, spring—maybe! I do so want to believe this! Oh, dear Lord, will the time of singing surely come again?

Tuesday, March 18

Kites and spring! The two are almost synonymous; they go together like bacon and eggs in the Southwest where the wind blows more than it does in windy Chicago!

It is kite-flying weather and as Happy and I walked in the park today we saw lots of children and parents and dogs—nearly all of whom seemed either to be flying kites or chasing them! There are many unusual ones this year, reminiscent of the beautiful bird-kites we first saw on the Copacabana Beach in Rio de Janeiro a long time ago. Fascinated by them, we brought several back with us for the children we knew—including ourselves!

One Easter holiday we took our kite to Virginia Beach, thinking it would be fun to re-create Copacabana Beach along our own Atlantic coast. But the day turned cold and disagreeable; the weather didn't cooperate with our aerial adventure plans. Somehow we never did fly our graceful Brazilian bird. I suppose it is at the bottom of some navy footlocker in the attic along with a lot of other half-forgotten mementos.

Remembering all these things helps me get through these spring-splendored days. But it also brings pain—and tears.

Wednesday, March 26

A friend, also recently widowed, told me that she and a group of widows have dinner together each evening, usually taking turns as hostess. Afterwards they play bridge. She says, for them, this is a good way to spend otherwise lonely evenings; but this is not for me. I don't want that kind of escape. I'd rather be alone than spend that much time with so many other widows! That many duplicates of misery could only intensify, rather than diminish, my own sense of loneliness. Of course, perhaps some may not be all that lonely, indeed never may have been. Still, I just don't feel that I belong to a "society of widowhood." I'm just not "one of *them*" I protest to myself, however illusory and self-deceptive I realize this to be.

I have learned many interesting things about this segment of our society—the widows. For example, we aren't its most popular members. Ask any of us. We make lots of people uncomfortable. We disturb their complacency. We too visibly remind them of the ephemeral quality of life and of the married state, the suggestion of which is quite unwelcome to many who view themselves as the always-marrieds. As Joe and I did, they anticipate occupying "twin wheelchairs," growing old together; they'd rather not think it might be otherwise.

Also, though people expect widows to grieve, it must not be *too* long, and above all, one really must not constantly make reference to one's deceased husband. "This is in very bad taste, my dear!" We are urged back into the persons we were before widowhood (i.e., "I'll be glad when Nita is *herself* again!"). This, of course, is impossible, unrealistic, and unkind. No wonder we often are a disappointment both to ourselves and to others.

Wednesday, April 2

I agree with the observation that what is most difficult to adjust to and what, more than anything else, causes us to mourn is becoming accustomed to the absence of the one who has died. That's just the trouble— one doesn't become accustomed to the absence! That awful chasm, that yawning emptiness grows, an endless void, swallowing and consuming one totally. Joe's absence is everywhere, an omnipresent influence in my life.

I close my eyes and feel his touch, that special quality of his skin—warm, sensual, inviting. I hear his voice; I experience the unique, very personal essence of his body. And I question, "What do people mean when they say 'time heals'?"

A friend called to reassure me, "I promise you, you *will* be happy again." It is difficult to believe her. It is far easier to concur with Edna St. Vincent Millay who wrote:

> Time does not bring relief; you all have lied
> Who told me time would ease me of my pain!

Right on, Vincie! Still, I shall be grateful if time does succeed in altering into something a bit more agreeable my present state of loneliness and need.

Sunday, April 6

At church this morning I wept for Joe and the emptiness of the pew beside me and the hand that is not there to reach out and hold.

On the back of my church bulletin I wrote:

IN THE SANCTUARY

I reach for your hand,
Those dear, warm fingers
That intertwined with mine
In prayer, in the sanctuary.

But the pew beside me is empty,
You are not here. No hand
Reaches out to clasp my hand.
No prayer mingles with mine at
    the Throne of Grace.

But wait! Is it possible,
Because you are there, united
With Him who answers prayer,
From whom all blessings flow;
My prayer, after all, is with
Yours; is heard, and answered
    as never before?

Thursday, April 10

Thank goodness, little Bird-Bird seems improved today. For days he sat with his head under his wing most of the time, crooning softly to himself. It seemed as if he sang not a song but a dirge; I exhausted every remedy my book on parakeets suggested, but to no avail. I was so afraid he would die! There it was again—a familiar fear. The thought of death, any death, invading my household again leaves me almost undone.

I understand more fully, I think, what C.S. Lewis meant when he wrote in *A Grief Observed*: "No one ever told me that grief felt so much like fear."

For me, there was first the fear that Joe would die, a fear that became all-encompassing, possessing me utterly. This was followed by a growing awareness that time was running out. Fear and grief became one, indistinguishable and indiscriminate. Finally, there was only grief. All that I had feared had come to pass. But, somehow, the two emotions had commingled, fused into one. Now death, in whatever form, reproduces in me this dread fear-grief that annihilates me totally.

This morning, Bird-Bird is preening himself and singing. His song scarcely could be sweeter to my ears if it were the "Hallelujah Chorus"! Is it possible that a similar transformation can turn *my* lament into laughter?

Saturday, April 12

Today I went to a nursery where I bought a dozen petunia plants, some geraniums, and several potted plants. Like Joe, I nearly got carried away and bought more than I could plant. He used to do this all of the time. I understand why; it is difficult not to buy everything in sight, because the look and feel of spring, and of growing things, is so overpowering. And rarely is this more so than at a nursery stocked with all of the season's most enticing specimens.

When reading, walking Happy, playing the piano and all else fails, I garden. There are few things that bring me more peace and equanimity than digging in the soil. And even I, who must have been born impatient, acquire a degree of patience in awaiting the results of my gardening efforts.

I think of the song, "There's a time for planting, a time for reaping. . . ." So now I plant; and I pray that the miracle of spring's promises will come into full fruition, not only in my garden but also in my life.

Monday, April 14

Death, that stealthy, stalking specter, strikes the great and the small. Last evening, my beautiful little Bird-Bird died.

I realized he wasn't singing during the day, but I attributed his silence to the dreary, rainy, gloomy day when even the birds outdoors hid from the weather.

While he lived he made a glad song and gave me much company and pleasure. I shall miss him very much. I am grateful to you, Lord, for creating such exquisite little feathered friends and for putting a song in their throats. And for your awareness when even a little bird dies.

About midnight we had a violent storm—much lightning, thunder, rain, and wind. In the midst of it, I thought I heard Bird-Bird singing! Impossible! I knew I didn't, couldn't! But I got up to check anyway. He was quite dead.

I returned to bed and wept for that stilled song, feeling once again very grief-stricken and bereft.

Thursday, April 17

Oh, dear Lord! Did you have to create such balmy spring days and nights? So much beauty that needs sharing? Until now, I suppose I would have defined loneliness as a state of mind, or of being. Tonight, it has an identity with the name of Joe!

I miss him until I ache with an emotion so overwhelming that it blots out all other feelings.

Today I saw a squirrel drinking from the birdbath under the breakfast room windows and I involuntarily cried, "Look, darling!"

Why cannot I come to terms with his absence? Accept the fact that he is dead? Oh, God, you tell me! What *am* I to do?

Wednesday, April 23

Joe gave me such confidence—now I haven't *any*! I did my job well, knowing I had his support and approval; I was a good homemaker and hostess because he thought there was nothing I couldn't do; I earned navy promotions because he expected me to and encouraged me. Now it seems I do nothing with any skill or grace. Last night, in class, I was as inarticulate as I ever recall being and I questioned, "Whatever became of my ability to communicate—an English major, journalist, public speaker—is it all gone?"

Earlier this week, at a meeting of church women—a delightful company of charming and friendly ladies—I felt as though I were an outsider. As is the case wherever I've been lately, I was the first to leave, escaping as quickly as possible into my self-imposed cocoon of security where I don't feel so alienated—at home, in the car, walking Happy. Especially walking Happy under an umbrella of stars or in the morning before the neighborhood is awake. These are the times and places in which I don't feel separated, apart.

This is absurd, I know. Yet, despite my realization of the unwholesomeness of such feelings, it sometimes seems that loneliness has become my only confidant.

I miss the person I used to be—gregarious, extroverted, alive, and happy!

Monday, April 28

After all my past avowals to the contrary, today I bought another little parakeet to replace Bird-Bird whom I miss so much! What a laugh at my expense Joe and his mother must be having! I, who had categorically denied I'd ever have a bird in my house—and who didn't really want B-B—had invited him to come to live with us when his mistress, Joe's mother, died. I was anything but gracious about this, as I remember to my shame. Little did I know how quickly he would sing his way into dominion of my heart!

The new one, whom I've named B-B Two, is a little boy bird only a few weeks old, still very shy and untamed. No doubt he misses his little feathered cousins who occupied the big cage with him at the pet shop; but in a few days I hope he will be entirely at home here with Happy and me.

I will remember you, mother and Joe, as B-B Two and I get acquainted and develop what I hope will be a long friendship. I am indebted to you both for insisting that we have a parakeet, the result of which is that another avenue of love for nature and for God's creation was opened up to me. I now understand so much better your need and love for your birds, mother. I hope you know that.

Tuesday, May 6

I read an article in which the author expressed the opinion that one of the most important things in a happy marriage is the opportunity to share things—both little and big—with someone who cares and to whom they matter as much as they do to you.

Elementary, my dear Watson! Any widow could have told you that! And she could have added that the most difficult thing about widowhood is that inability to share—and the knowledge that she is no longer really the most important person in the world to a single, solitary person! It is amazing how much that diminishes one!

A letter from a friend today suggests, "You need some new interests. The time has come for that. You have a lot to give and it is being wasted. You must try to get out more and mix more socially."

Good advice. I wish I knew how to follow it.

Tuesday, May 13

This evening I saw Venus and Mercury, luminously bright and visible just now. They are low in the western sky and appear quite near one another, though I know they are, in reality, millions of miles apart. What a memorable sight they were, and I immersed myself in their beauty—yet another majestic spectacle of the heavens. I thought, "What a creative, loving God we have to surround us with so many evidences of His caring and His sovereignty!"

I was overwhelmed with a sense of my own finiteness—my inadequacies, my faults and sins. I was especially overcome with an awful sadness and remorse that I failed to pray through the years for Joe's recovery as I should have prayed. Oh, yes, I did pray! But not without ceasing! Worse, my ever-present fears must have created an impenetrable barrier much too often!

Looking at Venus and Mercury I was reminded of the quotation, "I have loved the stars so long I shall not fear the night." I resolved, with God's help, never again to allow fear to control my life.

Wednesday, May 21

Today I read that Eleanor Roosevelt once said, "No one can make you feel inferior without your consent." One concludes this was a mature observation based, perhaps, upon her earlier experiences as a young girl whose self-esteem often was threatened.

Strangely, mine is a reverse experience to that of Mrs. Roosevelt. As a young woman, and even well beyond, I possessed a great deal of confidence—feelings of worth as an individual, and a belief in myself as a person of some talents and abilities. Now I am uncertain about all of these.

Do we "consent" to events, as well as people, controlling the way we feel about ourselves? I cannot dispute that; I only know that once I was confident and self-assured—indeed, I had the world by the tail, thought there was little I couldn't do. Now I am vulnerable and questioning.

I hardly know *me* anymore. I never considered—while he lived—that my identity was so interrelated with Joe's and I am certain he never wanted that for me—then or now. Somehow, I must re-establish in my mind the fact of my own personhood and that, as a child of God, I do have worth.

Monday, May 26

Memorial Day. Strangely, the place that comes most vividly to mind is not Hillcrest Memorial Park, though I do go there for prayer and meditation. (I am glad to find miniature American flags flying over many graves, including Joe's.)

Rather, the place that, more than any other, is synonymous with Memorial Day for me is Arlington National Cemetery, a hallowed and very special spot to many of us who spent part of our lives in military service as both Joe and I did. On one of my active duty assignments in Washington, I could look out my office windows and observe a military funeral in progress almost daily. For me, those were sacred moments, and there is scarcely a more appropriate memorial ceremony. Joe and I used to say we wanted to be buried in Arlington, but that was when we lived nearby and visited the shrine regularly. Many of our friends are buried there.

One often hears the cliché, "It doesn't matter *how long* one lives, but *how.*"

Ridiculous! Of course it matters—terribly! Who can say it didn't matter to all of those young men and women who lost their lives as a result of our nation's wars? Death, whenever it comes, always matters!

How did such a meaningless axiom ever get started? It has no validity whatever, especially on this Memorial Day.

Tuesday, June 3

Today someone whose love and friendship mean a great deal to me asked, "How are you?"

Truthfully I replied, "Oh, pretty good."

"No, you're not! You're *fine!*" he demanded, denying both my honest response and my need to convey to a caring person that I really am not faring too well.

No, people do not expect or want to hear the truth when they inquire, "How are you?" Any admission other than "fine" might call for an investment of some kind on the part of the inquirer—an involvement for which he is unprepared.

I must remember this and hereafter answer such questions perfunctorily and with little candor.

Sunday, June 8

The gardenias are in bloom, wafting many poignant memories my way as I admire their fragrant, velvety white blossoms.

They remind me, first of all, of mama who grew them in great profusion and called them by the old-fashioned name of Cape Jessamine. One of my earliest memories is of rocking gently back and forth in the front porch swing and being intoxicated with the perfume of these flowers and by the beauty all around me. Mama's flower garden was, to my child's mind, a veritable Garden of Eden, as it remains in my memory.

The gardenias remind me of Hawaii where their fragrance fills the balmy night air. And, of course, they remind me of Joe. What thing of beauty does not?

When we moved to Texas and bought our house, I passionately wanted "one of everything that grew in Mama's garden," and Joe patiently indulged me in this wish. I remember quite well the day he brought home a small lilac bush, which said "April!" to me, and three gardenia bushes. We planted all with great care and watched over them with loving concern. The following year we were rewarded with a few lilacs (we later learned lilacs will hardly grow in our black gumbo soil) and with quite a number of gardenias. I was ecstatic!

Joe spotted the first gardenia on my birthday and gravely presented it to me as though it were an exquisite jewel which, in truth, it was! Each year, thereafter, we always hoped the gardenia bushes would be in bloom on my birthday and they often were.

After we had been here a few years and he was

recuperating from his initial heart attack, Joe was offered a very attractive and exciting position on the East Coast where we had previously lived. As much as we enjoyed living in Texas and loved our home, he was tempted to accept the job. I assured him the decision was his; I was quite willing to live wherever he felt his career and personal happiness lay. Nevertheless, the thought of leaving this place, into which we had put so much of ourselves along with lots of hard work, saddened us both.

One evening as we walked Happy, we tried to consider all of the pros and cons of the job offer. The pros got the nod; he really must accept it. We were in total agreement and I remember saying something like, "Oh, darling, home is where we are together. We'll have another house that we like as much as we do this one." High-sounding sentiment, but I meant it.

As we rounded the corner on our block, the first thing I saw was our brave little lilac bush trying very hard to grow in its less than hospitable environment. Suddenly it represented everything that meant home and security and an end to the sometimes rootless navy years. And I thought, "How can I leave that lilac bush? I cannot possibly allow someone else to watch it struggle to grow and to enjoy its beauty when we've worked so hard here!"

I said nothing, but tears, unbidden, came to my eyes and Joe was quick to see them. Quietly he squeezed my hand and asked, "Is something wrong, angel?"

I replied, "I think I got a speck in my eye."

On the pretext of washing my eye out, I hurried into the house, and into the shower—where I had my cry. The subject of moving wasn't mentioned again that evening.

As it developed, we didn't move, after all, but remained in my beloved Texas and in the house which meant so much to us both.

From time to time, however, whenever I was sad or weepy throughout the ensuing years, Joe would inquire, "Did you get a speck in your *eye,* darling?"

The gardenias are in bloom. A few days late for my birthday. Yes, I have another "speck in my *eye.*"

Friday, June 13

"Why aren't you doing something? Why don't you get involved in volunteering or another job? Do something constructive!" Longtime friends have again taken me to task for living too much in the past, for not giving a better accounting of myself.

"You're only interested in Happy and your house. What in the world do you do with yourself all day? Don't you ever think of the future?" Questions like these hammer away at my flagging self-confidence.

Dear God, cannot they understand that all I can muster is today? That it takes all of my resources just to *be*? What have I left over for others? Okay, this is entirely selfish, introverted, and sickeningly self-pitying. No argument there. Hardly worse, however, than friends usurping this prerogative to so knowingly tell me how to act, to think, to be. How are they so sure what is right for me?

And, of course, "You must remarry some day!" Always and always the subject of marriage is raised as though that must be uppermost in my mind and also that there are countless suitable prospects ringing one's doorbell. Most widows would say neither is true.

I love my friends; but their advice, however well intentioned, only makes me defensive. The more threatened I feel, the more intense and outspoken I also become. Its been called "coming on strong" when I vehemently reject their proffered advice. We all suffer as a consequence and I think, "There *must* be a better way!"

Tuesday, June 17

The day, though beautiful, started out wrong. As Happy and I began our walk, I thought, once again, of our friend's beautiful basset hound which had been cruelly and inhumanely destroyed. At that time, I cried for the beautiful dog, and I was bitterly angry at the owner. These emotions are evoked each time I remember that sad day.

At just the moment I was remembering that basset hound, a little female dog darted out into the street ahead of us and a car hit her. I knew immediately that she had been injured though she didn't cry. By the time I reached her, she was going round and round in a circle but I managed to pick her up and hold her until her owner arrived to claim her. She was badly injured, I was sure—too hurt to cry or so stunned that she could not.

My tears began to flow in earnest and I have cried all day. Somehow, I just haven't been able to stop, though I realize this has distressed Happy who keeps trying to comfort me as though he feels responsible for my sorrow. I have petted and reassured him. And I have spent hours working in the yard, usually a balm to my wounded spirits. But today nothing has brought relief.

I feel as if I have been mortally wounded—that my tears will forever flow. I am once again a sad, tear-stained child sent "outside to cry so no one will hear."

This evening, the owner told me the little dog had died.

Saturday, June 21

Last evening two friends and I attended a concert by Tony Bennett, a favorite performer of mine and Joe's whose concerts we often attended in years gone by. The program contained all of the old favorites we had danced to and loved—and I felt you close to me, darling.

Later, at home, I could not sleep. Putting on a robe, I went into the library where an almost-full moon was shining brightly through the bay windows. I turned on the hi-fi and, in the moonlight, I sat and listened to beautiful music. For hours I sat there, remembering the feel of you with your body fitting so close to mine and the sound and scent of you pervading the room. And I thought, "Even if, with my mind, I could forget you, my heart and the blood it sends pulsing through my body would remember!"

Lines from Walter Benton's poem, "Jones Beach" came to mind:

Love is a burden if you cannot give it,
O hoarded love is heavy to bear.

Dear Mr. Benton, how graphically you describe my feelings and this burden of love I carry, with no one upon whom to bestow it!

Summer officially began today. What can a new season say that autumn, winter, spring already have not said?

48

Sunday, July 6

Wow! That was some storm we had this evening! Lightning, rain, wind, hail—for a while, it seemed there might be a lot of damage as a result of it all, but eventually it passed over, leaving little local destruction in its wake.

Neither Happy nor I like storms; but I am not nearly so fearful of them as I once was. I used to really hate them and fear them but Joe saw them as beautiful, another revelation of the majesty and glory of God. He liked to reminisce about the way he and fellow navy pilots flew their flimsy, early World War II aircraft into big thunderheads, chasing one another in and out of the cloud cover. He always felt a thrill at being one with the wind and sky.

He had a remarkable way of making almost everything beautiful and interesting—and a challenge. Whatever the circumstances—outwardly at least—he always seemed calm. Thus, despite my own apprehension during storms, he had a calming effect upon me.

I cannot claim to have been entirely at ease at the height of today's storm. Indeed, I had already made a mental note of just how quickly I could gather Bird-Bird, Happy, and me into the big hall closet if this seemed indicated. But, neither was I really afraid. Progress, darling?

Friday, July 11

A cherished friend invited me and several other guests to a delicious and beautifully served dinner. Afterwards we played bridge.

But oh, what *am* I going to do? There we were—all dressed up in party dresses and jewels. The conversation consisted mostly of grandchildren (I haven't any), the price of food, recipes, and clothes. Why do women so often engage in such uninteresting chatter?

I am frantic when I realize that this is the sort of social event to which I am likely to be invited from now on. No more unwilling subject than I could be found for this and I suspect that, instead of accepting, more and more I shall retreat into my house, pets, books, and music, however introverted and inappropriate this may be.

Oh, dear God, I miss Joe so much—not only him, but also the interesting life we lived together when we traveled, entertained, went to virtually all of the performing arts events, and danced! We used to enjoy, equally, two-handed gin rummy, picnics and football games. We had lots of house guests—family and otherwise. We *did* things! Now none of these seem to happen often; I can't go through the rest of my life avoiding social encounters, but I can't be "one of the girls" either!

I am lost in a forest of loneliness, a world in which I am almost a stranger. Yet I reject so much that is proffered me! How do I go about making the "adjustment to this other life" everyone suggests? Nobody tells me how.

Saturday, July 19

Bird-Bird Two has repaid my presence in the kitchen most of today with an almost constant display of his acrobatic and vocal talents! He has gone through his entire repertoire of songs and has said, over and over, all of the words he knows—"Hello, my name is Bird-Bird! Good morning, where's Happy?" I've been both amused and delighted with his happy accompaniment to my chores.

He loves it when there is lots of activity—the more, the better. If Happy is barking, demanding attention, and I'm talking to him; or if I'm typing, using the mixer, vacuum cleaner, or just about any other noisemaker, he is absolutely elated. And joins in the general din and confusion.

But today, more than anything, he has sung and sung and it has gladdened my heart. It is almost as though he is saying, "It is nice to have you here with me today, therefore I shall serenade you."

It is good to have singing in the house. Mama often sang as she went about her daily tasks and dad, too, sang as he did his chores. I grew up with music and song and often have been told I tried to sing "Joy Bells" before I scarcely could talk. I rarely sing any more, except for hymns at church. Like Bird-Bird, I guess I, too, sang better and more often when there was someone to share my efforts and to join in the merrymaking.

Sunday, July 20

Happy routed me out of bed early this morning and took me on a delightful chase through Greenway Parks and down by the tennis courts. We haven't walked that way in months but Happy definitely remembers this favorite route, and could not be prevented from going in that direction. I wonder what else he remembers but cannot communicate to me?

As we returned home I tossed a neighbor's newspaper on her porch and, seeing me, she came out to thank me.

"My husband and I used to watch for the three of you to come by on your walks. You seemed so happy. We've missed you," she said. She added a number of other very nice things about us, and especially Joe, who was a neighborhood favorite. It pleased me so much.

Turning this encounter over in my mind I thought, "It takes so little to add a 'cup of sunshine' to another's life. Why cannot we all do this more often?"

I hope that neighbor knows how much she brightened my day!

Tuesday, July 22

As I gardened today one of the little squirrels that Joe trained to come to him for pecans also came up to me. He ran very near and then sat back on his little haunches and started to chatter. I said, "I don't have any pecans" and started to walk away. But he would have none of it! He insistently came closer, close enough to scratch my slacks leg. I told him, "Wait a minute; I'll get you some lunch," and went into the garage where I keep the pecans, the squirrel following expectantly all the while.

He took the nuts from my hand, one at a time, confident that as he consumed one I was standing there with another. He ate his fill, ever so carefully, so that he didn't drop a single morsel—and completely finished one pecan before reaching for the next.

This little episode made me feel strangely close to Joe and somehow less lonely. As I mulled it over, the thought came to me, "I wish I could exhibit the confidence of that squirrel, that I could always be that trusting."

Sunday, July 27

As Happy and I went for a walk this evening there were beautiful pink, mauve, and orange hues in the western sky, dominating the horizon. They were a glorious and heavenly sight, a foretaste of the coming kingdom.

The display this evening reminded me of another beautiful sky—perhaps the most beautiful I ever saw, even including a memorable display of the aurora borealis one night (or early morning, really) as we flew into Minneapolis from Chicago. Once, Joe and I were driving back into Dallas and as we topped the hill just before reaching Lake Ray Hubbard, everywhere we looked the sky was filled with color—the same oranges, pinks, and mauves that I saw this evening—unique cloud formations and sunbursts streaming behind them from a lowering sun. Fingers of color stretched skyward and back to earth again, filtering light and magic all along the expanse of sky. It was an unforgettable picture.

Enthralled, we said to one another, "This must be the way heaven looks," remembering Renaissance painters who often made the sky look ethereal. I wonder, darling, *does* it look like that from where you are?

Wedneday, August 6

Today I listened to some Bach concertos and read. Music and books—they have been my life these past months. I remembered something I once read, "A book should serve as an axe for the frozen sea within us." I agree. How I've needed something to dislodge the glacial block into which I've been encased and to return to some semblance of my former self.

I have felt exiled, cut off from all that means most to me. Sometimes I am really quite horrified by a terrible realization of what I am becoming: a frightened, introverted, lonely, and reclusive person, avoiding people even as I need them. The antithesis of the way I've always been—and unable to escape this unwanted destiny.

I understand, I think, why some people, under similar circumstances, develop unwise emotional attachments, become alcoholics, or engage in other foolish and destructive behavior. It is to avoid a world in which they feel alien and to try to create a world in which, in anonymity perhaps, they can survive.

It is possible, I believe, that alone with my books and music I am less lonely, more my own person, than some who try to find security in a familiar, hidebound routine; or others who endlessly divert themselves with feverish group activity, avoiding any time whatever to be alone with their own thoughts.

On the other hand, I also may be masochistically seeking loneliness while simultaneously protesting how lonely I am. If so, how ironic—and what a waste!

Tuesday, August 12

I saw J. today and was reminded of the evening, soon after Joe's death, when she invited me to join our church choir. She even came by and took me to rehearsal. The choir members and the director, a good friend, were very welcoming and gracious.

Their ultimate kindness was their voluntary tone deafness in reaction to the sour notes I hit.

Sing!? I could scarcely breathe. Every hymn and anthem on the rehearsal schedule was sadder and more doleful than the last. And the lump in my throat, bigger and bigger as the evening progressed, threatened to prevent my ever using my voice again, even to speak—much less sing. Clearly, the evening was a disaster for me.

On the way home I began to cry and I told J., "I guess I'm not ready for the choir, after all."

I love to sing. But I've not been back.

Friday, August 15

I go for my annual physical and the doctor tells me, "You must undergo major surgery immediately. My nurse will make arrangements for your prompt admission to the hospital and I'll perform the surgery Monday morning."

I say, "Okay," get in my car, and start driving. But I do not go home. Instead, I drive to Hillcrest Memorial Park—to Joe's grave. I sit on the bench under a beautiful old oak tree that shades the site. It is peaceful, quiet, serene there—a good place to try to collect my thoughts, to put meaning into the doctor's pronouncement, to plan for the hospital stay. Mostly, I just sit there, immobile, part of the marble statuary. Blank, unseeing, unfeeling.

Eventually, I return to my car, drive home, walk Happy.

Does the surgery frighten me? I don't think so. Not really. But being hospitalized alone does. Who is there to care? Who will be with me before I go into surgery, waiting for my return?

Silly! Thousands of other people do this all of the time. But I'm not one of those people. I'm *me*. It is my first trip to the hospital without Joe. And I need him.

Thursday, August 21

How could I have forgotten how kind, how caring people really can be? So many dear friends have surrounded me with their love, their prayers, their presence during this hospital stay.

Nor was I alone before or after surgery. How can I ever express my profound gratitude to all of those who had said, more eloquently than mere words, "We do care, and we are here"?

It has been *almost* enjoyable—to see so many people whom I really like a lot and from whom I hadn't heard recently. During these past months of feeling sorry for myself, and of isolating myself from even old and dear friends, I had almost lost track of some of them; yet here they are, popping in to say hello and showing their concern. I *am* profoundly grateful—for that, and also for making such a rapid recovery.

To my surprise, I have rediscovered a *joie de vivre* that I thought no longer existed; I had thought it could not be resurrected. Amazing! One need only be incapacitated for even a short while to realize that life—and health—are rather precious commodities, after all, however much I may have spurned at least the former these past months.

Tuesday, August 26

I came across a short story about a man with a heart condition whose wife, as I did, lived in great fear. Despite his precarious health, the man insisted upon going into the wilds of Mexico to continue research activities. While there he suffered a heart attack, even as his wife had feared.

A Mexican woman asked the wife why her husband, if he were so ill, would come to such a place.

The wife answered that he had always done so. To simply sit would be opening the door to death. The Mexican woman then understood: he preferred to go out to meet it.

The story ended with an old Mexican proverb: Take what you want from life—and pay for it.

I now remembered something significant: Some years ago when Floyd (my eldest brother) was dying of cancer, Joe had said to me, "If ever I am terminally ill, I do not want to spend my final days in a hospital. I'd prefer to go fishing. Let death find me with a fishing rod in my hands, out in the fresh air and sunshine, by some quiet stream."

Why had I not recalled this conversation of the past—this wish of Joe's—until now?

At last, I finally understood his compelling need to go fishing that last weekend just before he died, though we both knew I was terrified for him to go. Sensing that death was near, he preferred to keep his rendezvous with destiny holding a fishing rod in his hands rather than sitting and waiting for death to come. Like the man in the story, he didn't quibble about the price.

I, on the other hand, tried to bargain with God for him—and lost, while Joe accepted with equanimity and serenity what seemed inevitable. And what, of course, must, in time, come to us all. For me, his impending death was a never-ending crisis; for him it must have become, if not welcome, at least something he did not dread.

Oh, I wish I had found a way to rise above my fear as Joe did and that I'd had as much courage. As he did, I wish I, too, could have gone on doing what gave the largest dimension to life, conquering instead of being conquered.

Thursday, September 4

Recuperation. For the first time, I think, I have a small awareness of how Joe must have felt at times: too well to stay in bed all day; too weak to do much. Energies quickly expended so that even short walks with Happy tire me out. Hungry, but for what? Wish for someone to just talk with. Oh, so thankful to be improving but it seems so slow! Will I never feel any better, have any more energy than now?

I don't write or play the piano, or even read, as much as I usually do. A malaise settles over me, covering me like a blanket.

Now I understand Joe's need to get out, almost anywhere, some of the evenings, a diversion from the long hours spent in inactivity and alone. Whereas I, exhausted from my job, longed for nothing quite so much as the peace and quiet of home. Oh, how I wish I had understood better how it is to be convalescing.

We communicated so well about almost everything—yet when we should have understood one another perfectly, it seems I did not fully know how much he needed a change from those long, lonely hours of being cooped up in the house, away from former associates and friends, and the exciting demands of a creative career. But I *should* have. And the knowledge that I did not fills me with a futile and awful sorrow.

Friday, September 12

Turning on the FM radio or playing tapes or records is almost as automatic for me, and as constant, as breathing. One or the other is nearly always on from the moment I awaken until I fall asleep at night. I used to wonder why Joe did this; the mystery has been unraveled now.

Today I heard a very beautiful, unfamiliar melody—a new love song of longing and fulfillment. I thought, "By whatever name, darling, they are playing 'our song.'" It saddened me momentarily to realize that Joe, an ardent music lover, never heard this particular composition that I liked so much and identified with so quickly. Then it came to me: But *he* also is hearing music—inexpressibly beautiful music—that *I* have never heard! The melody I heard today is but a clanging cymbal compared with the music Joe is now enjoying.

Tuesday, September 16

My longing for Joe and my need of him this day has been literally physical! It is a compelling, unrelenting thing, driving all else from my consciousness, and it will not let me go.

I am a woman who needs her man—at least I can be honest enough with myself to admit this. Without him, I'm faceless, functionless, unfulfilled. Oh, dear Lord, this is what it feels like not to be a woman at all!

With Carl Sandburg, I cry, "But leave me a little love!" Some time ago I memorized his poem, "At a Window":

Give me hunger,
O you gods that sit and give
The world its orders.
Give me hunger, pain and want,
Shut me out with shame and failure
From your doors of gold and fame,
Give me your shabbiest, weariest hunger!

But leave me a little love,
A voice to speak to me in the day end,
A hand to touch me in the dark room
Breaking the long loneliness.

I haven't wept for a long time now; today I need to shed tears that will not fall.

Saturday, September 20

I found an interesting cartoon by Alex Graham of that lovable English basset hound, Fred Basset. Fred's mistress is talking to him as she does her chores and he observes in all of his basset hound wisdom: "She chats away to me all day. Of course, she has nobody else to speak to, and I'm a very good listener!"

Fred, you took the words right out of Happy's mouth! I'm sure he thinks the same thoughts; he is so perceptive and understanding of my every word, mood, and action.

Joe's mother used to hold conversations with him, even though he might be nowhere near. I thought it was endearing and amusing—an attribute of her advancing years. Now I understand her need to share with him was so great that she did so, whether or not he was within earshot. These days I do the same thing. I believe actual communication may well be taking place.

Tuesday, September 23

Tonight I sat in the unlighted library, enjoying the moonlight streaming in through the window and remembering summer nights when, as children, we sat with mama and dad on the front porch at home. Those were such special times! Nearly always there was the fragrance of flowers in the evening air: honeysuckle, roses, gardenias, sweet peas, wisteria. Mama's flower garden was always fragrant and beautiful.

Suddenly, inexplicably, my reverie was interrupted by an urge to turn on the lamps and take from a library shelf an old, almost-forgotten poetry scrapbook I had begun as a young girl. I cannot remember the last time I had even glanced through that book—it must have been years! Yet here I was, reaching for it as though responding to some inaudible command.

Almost immediately I saw a piece of paper with mama's distinctive handwriting on it. To my joy, I began reading a poem she had written to me when I was sixteen years old! I had searched over and over for that poem, could not locate it, and supposed it was irretrievably lost. But here it was! It was as though mama's voice from the past spoke to me through that poem and as I read once again her beautiful expression of love for me, I was overwhelmed with a sense of her presence. It was such a special moment!

Oh, thank you, mama, for having loved me enough to write such words of love and praise to me so long ago. This poem fills my soul this night with a quiet sense of belonging—and of peace.

Wednesday, October 1

This is our wedding anniversary and I awakened with the resolution: This day I *will* be happy, holding in a close embrace the memory of us and the love and laughter we shared.

I have rambled through scrapbooks and photograph albums, taking a mental voyage through the past, seeing us as we were then. Places, events—all the things we shared are inextricably woven into the fabric of us and our years together, the remembrance of which fills my heart with gladness.

The happy sound I hear is the voice of beautiful memories echoing through my mind. These are no discordant notes, only melodies of love and promise and joy on this anniversary day.

And all day, beloved, I have felt your presence. You have "sat on my shoulder," as you promised you would, if ever you should leave me, reminding me of all the marvelous and wonderful things wrought by our love.

The final benediction to the day came as Happy and I went for our evening walk. A perfect, golden autumn leaf fluttered and fell at my feet—a nostalgic reminder of "Autumn Leaves" and that autumn is our season, Joe.

Monday, October 13

I heard a speaker say, "I've found I usually can recall some verse of Scripture that meets nearly all of my needs."

A friend remarked, "I've never felt so close to God as I have since my husband died."

C.S. Lewis asks in *A Grief Observed:* "Can I meet H. again only if I learn to love you [God] so much that I don't care whether I meet her or not?"

Today I mulled over all three of these, and I discovered none fits me. Though not nearly as well as I should be, still I am pretty well acquainted with the Scriptures and yet I cannot always think of one that seems especially suited to my needs.

I feel God's nearness at times, but my highest mountain-top spiritual experiences thus far in my life were those shared with Joe. And the truth is, I've had more difficulty "finding God" since Joe's death than I ever remember having before. Looking too hard, perhaps?

Nor can I imagine God expecting that I not care whether I meet Joe again! The point, I believe, that C.S. Lewis was making was that our love of God must transcend *all* other loves. No disagreement there. Nevertheless, for me, being in God's presence in the hereafter also means being with Joe.

I cannot think of it any other way

Saturday, October 18

Today, like a huntress, I have stalked the house from room to room in search of something—or someone. A long, lonely Saturday spent rather restlessly and fruitlessly, I'm afraid.

Our favorite season, autumn, is here, darling. And there is no one with whom to share its bright, blue days! No one with whom to enjoy the many-hued autumn leaves, to go on a cookout with, to watch a football game. No one to whom I can say, "Oh, look at that squirrel!" as it hurries from tree to ground, and back to tree, with nuts in its fat little jaws, diligently storing food for winter. No one with whom to watch a rising harvest moon, huge and golden. No one to love.

It is the totally frustrating inability to share all of the little things that make up a day: the exhilarating walk with Happy on crisp, cool mornings, the first cup of coffee, the morning paper. The days come and go and except for salespeople (is this why lonely people aimlessly shop so much?), the occasional telephone call, and the neighbors I see on walks, I hardly talk to anyone all day.

These autumn days and nights are as beautiful as any I remember in recent years. As I walked Happy early this morning the moon still was shining almost as brightly as it had been when we walked last evening. It is a double bonus to see it shining so beautifully at both the beginning and the end of the day.

Camus wrote, ". . . there is only misfortune in not being loved; there is misery in not loving." For me, the misery extends to them both. Oh, how I miss not being loved—and not loving!

OCTOBER PRAYER

O Lord, recall a myriad of stars,
Veil the moon, becloud the sky.
You have blessed us with too much beauty;
Your world, this night, is far too marvelous.

Heaven, not earth, should be perfect,
Lord. Take some of this brilliance from us.
Thy bountiful hand has been over-generous,
It is too much for human eye to behold.

Another night of equal splendor, of
October's wine-scented gardens and fields;
And like Lot's wife who turned to look again,
I, too, will be tempted to linger here.

Monday, October 27

I am taking another trip and here I go again, a yo-yo on a string! Up, I want to go; down, I'd prefer to stay at home. Up, yes; down, no. One moment I'm excited about going, the next I wonder what ever possessed me to plan another journey. I am a puzzle to myself; no wonder I am an enigma to others as well.

It is the leaving home I do not like. Happy misses me, for one thing, and it is difficult to arrange for his and Bird-Bird's care. Then, it is another leave-taking for which I am unprepared. I've had too many of those in the past months—so many good-byes that became so final!

As the time draws near for me to leave, I become something of the little girl I once was, prompting mama by saying, "Regardless of how much I beg you to let me spend the night, please say no!" before my little friend and I came to ask. I couldn't admit to my friend I didn't want to go; I can't always do so now. But the truth is, I guess, I really want to be home "when night comes." Symbolically and actually.

I hope my loved and loving family and friends never learn about this feeling of ambivalence, which I cannot fully explain. I do appreciate their invitations and, once I am with them in their homes, I have a very good time.

Monday, November 3

Today I went shopping for a new dress as none of the many dresses hanging in my closets is long enough, now that the new, longer style is in vogue.

I found a beautiful three-piece silk gabardine suit with a much longer skirt that is gored and flared. The jacket is lavishly trimmed in fox fur, dyed to match the blue of the gabardine material. The *pièce de résistance* is a matching chiffon blouse with long sleeves and a generous bow tie at the neckline. It is all very feminine and womanly and seductive in the most refined and ladylike manner. I loved it!

But my reaction: Why am *I* looking at this beautiful and luxurious outfit? It is too dressy, too stylish—for a *widow*! How absurd! And yes, sad! *Why* should such a thought have come to mind at all? Joe delighted in my wearing pretty and feminine things and often chose them for me. The suit, becoming and really beautiful, was something he might very well have selected. And it could have been worn for many occasions. Therefore, the obvious question: What possible connection was there between my being a widow and whether or not I purchased the suit?

Nevertheless, I didn't buy it. Instead, I bought a simple, unadorned, tailored dress, telling myself, "You'll get more wear from this." But why? *Why?*

Friday, November 7

A prayer has been answered; finally I have dreamed a happy, marvelous, wonderful dream about Joe in which he was well, perfectly natural, and his handsome, extroverted self! Not a hint of the terrifying dreams I've had so often in which he always seems to be having a heart attack and all is pain, darkness, and endless hopelessness.

The dream began with his telephoning me, and it was like old times when he used to call me from wherever the ship docked or the plane landed.

Later, he appeared in his navy uniform, looking exactly as he had looked then—and oh, what a joyous homecoming we had!

The dream ended with his holding his arms out to me, open wide, and I ran into them and was enveloped in his strong embrace. I experienced a feeling of happiness and security I have not known since his death. Oh, I am so glad to have had this dream!

Can it be that I've finally emerged from that dark tunnel of despair in which the other dreams entrapped me? *That* would *really* be an answer to prayer! Dear God, let it be so.

Tuesday, November 18

As I dressed for bed I looked out the bathroom window and observed that the predicted eclipse of the moon had begun. I stood, transfixed, watching as first only a tiny portion, then more, and more—and finally, virtually all of the moon had been blotted from sight. The earth was in shadows.

How quickly it happened! I don't know how long I watched this fascinating process but it seemed like only minutes. Then it was over; once again the shadows were dissipated by the moon's bright light.

It was a moving experience and I felt privileged to be an observer of this celestial spectacle.

In humility I prayed that God would help me to believe, even as the shadows over the earth from the moon's eclipse quickly disappeared, so shall the shadows that darken my life. And that I will be led out of the temporary darkness of these present days back into the sunshine of His marvelous light.

Friday, November 21

Last night, about eleven o'clock, I was reading in bed when suddenly I heard the honk, honk, honk of geese flying south. I listened. Yes, the sound was unmistakable! I jumped up and ran outside, Happy with me. Despite a full moon and a night that was almost as light as day, I could not spot the familiar V. I was disappointed; but the sound, now growing more faint, was still audible. I knew that somewhere in the starry sky those geese had their long, graceful necks pointed southward toward a timeless rendezvous, synchronized with the seasonal clock of the universe.

What memories of childhood this evoked! Mama and dad, ever alert to all of nature's beauties and surprises, used to call to us, "Hurry, children, come see the geese flying south," almost every year.

There is something primeval, eternal about that beautiful formation and the unerring sense of direction and purpose these birds have as year after year they presage winter by their southward flights.

How can I question the mysteries of life when, every year, on schedule, there are miracles like wild geese flying south?

Thursday, November 27

A few days ago I answered the telephone to hear the voice of a loved friend: "We have tickets for ourselves and you to attend a performance of the Berlin Opera Company at the John F. Kennedy Center for the Performing Arts on Thanksgiving Day. You must come and go with us!"

How many, many times have these same wonderful friends included me in some special event, invited me to visit in their beautiful home, shared a holiday that would have been a lonely time otherwise, given freely of their advice and love?

Someone has said that to have only a few friends is to be rich. Well, I consider myself exceedingly blessed in having these two who, for almost thirty years, have befriended me in more ways, and under more circumstances, than I could possibly remember.

So here I am, spending yet another Thanksgiving Day with them, and enjoying a truly magnificent operatic evening at the beautiful JFK Center.

Chalk up another memorable day for which I am indebted to you, Sara Mae and Louis. I wonder if you have any idea how much I love and appreciate you both?

Wednesday, December 3

The sun has played hide-and-seek behind a scattering of clouds today and a chilling breeze has developed, reminding me that winter cannot be far off. As I walked Happy I smelled the tantalizing aroma of a wood fire in someone's fireplace and I thought that I, too, would like to rush the season a bit by having a fire in the library fireplace this evening. There is something very companionable and comforting about a fire in the fireplace!

I'd welcome a bit of comforting. This has been a restless day. And once again, all too feverishly and demandingly, I have asked God what I am to do with myself, what He wants me to accomplish for the remainder of my time here.

How foolishly I have prayed! God does not provide a blueprint for the rest of our lives! And, of course, I don't really want Him to! How thankful I am that He does not reveal the future to us. It is knowledge that I, for one, couldn't cope with—as He knows. It *should* be sufficient to accept the fact that we are in His keeping and that He knows and controls the future. Why is it that I always need everything all neatly laid out, catalogued and tabulated?

I think, in fairness to myself, what I have meant to be asking is for more purpose in my life than the aimless way I've spent so much of it these past months. No doubt the divine signposts have been put there for me to read. I've always been a poor navigator—"the world's worst," Joe used to say—so I haven't seen them or heeded them. Perhaps a better prayer would be, "What is your will for me without Joe—not for forever, but just for today?"

Friday, December 12

Christmas approaches. Because I won't be home for the holidays I have decorated the house early—not much fun alone, certainly not the ceremonial occasion it used to be with Joe creating a spectacular work of art on the tree, and then our drinking a toast of eggnog! Nevertheless, it is done. The tree is trimmed, the nativity scene is in place; and my favorite Christmas decoration of all, red-berried holly in polished silver containers, announces Christmas in a very special way. I have addressed and mailed the cards, wrapped the packages and I've listened to the carols which fill the musical airways.

All is the same, and nothing is the same—except in my memories. Oh, I miss the hustle and bustle of last-minute preparations, of Joe and his mother shopping right through the day of Christmas Eve; the secrecy of packages and the growing excitement of it all as Christmas Day draws near.

I miss the Christmas stockings with names inscribed, hanging from the mantel. I remember the year we added a stocking, stuffed with all sorts of doggie goodies, for Happy; he kept trying to investigate and sniff at it! I miss the family feel of Christmas, family prayers and worship.

And I miss getting dressed up and being pretty and feminine, smelling good and yes, being seductive. I miss the feeling of being a "girl-girl" as Joe liked me to be. I miss the me I was because of his love and I mind not being the most important person in the world to someone.

Probably these are inappropriate subjects on which my mind dwells as this holy season approaches. Surely they are not the most important! Of course I do think of God, and His Son, our Lord, whose birth gives significance and meaning not only to this season but to all of life. I thank God for His inestimable gift. I join in singing praises to His name. Christmas is very holy to me.

Still, in all candor, more than anything else this night, I miss Joe and the way he made not only holidays but every day memorable for me. I miss his love and his touch. My feelings are well described in these lines by Emily Dickenson:

Love is more than knowledge
And a woman withers without it.

Yes, Christmas is more than a season. It also is love, belonging, sharing. Without these it is incomplete.

Wednesday, December 17

Today is the anniversary of the historic flight of the Wright Brothers in Kitty Hawk, North Carolina, a date of special significance to Joe who had a lifelong love affair with aviation. He was particularly fascinated with man's first efforts to fly and, each year while on active navy duty, he joined other aviators and those in the aircraft industry in honoring the memory and achievements of Orville and Wilbur Wright.

Pan American's Clipper ships, the first planes to fly a regularly scheduled run from the United States to South America, were like graceful birds that flew right into his heart and nested there. He vowed that sometime he would be identified with this challenging and compelling industry and that he (at the time a performing artist with no technological background or training) would fly for Pan American.

Well, he did fly. He became a naval aviator during World War II and for the next twenty-one years he flew an assortment of navy planes. And, eventually, he also worked for Pan American, though not, as he had wished, as a pilot. Upon retirement from the navy he was employed as a public relations representative for Pan American.

Through the years, more often than not, Joe's for-entertainment reading was about aviation. Col. Charles A. Lindbergh was a special favorite, but he also made a detailed study of World War I aviation. Members of the Lafayette Escadrille, Capt. Eddie Rickenbacker, Baron Manfred von Richthofen (The Red Baron) and others of that day became familiar personalities to him.

Browsing in an art gallery one day, he spotted a sculpture of a World War I aviator and his wrecked plane. The piece, about thirty inches high, is authentic in every detail: the pilot, dressed in helmet with goggles, scarf, jacket, flying breeches and boots, even wears twin pistols, one holstered on each leg. The plane, badly damaged and resting on its fusilage, obviously has been shot down in combat. The rakish pilot, one foot balanced on the wing tip, is tossing a brave salute skyward. The title given the sculpture by its artist is "Au Revoir."

For reasons I cannot fully comprehend Joe was entranced with this work of art. The piece isn't, to my mind, all that beautiful although I do appreciate the artistry and imagination that went into the work. He wanted it so much! When I suggested that he purchase it, he said it was too expensive.

Nevertheless, he frequented the gallery regularly and always spent some time visiting with his old friend, the aviator! Always he would ask the gallery owner, "Has anyone bought my friend?" and was relieved each time she assured him the piece was still for sale.

A few months prior to Joe's death, I felt a strange compulsion to give him this sculpture which I had not even seen, but about which he had spoken so often. To the delight of both of us, I did so and as he hurried to the gallery for his aviator I knew this extravagance—if indeed it be that—was the right thing to have done.

That evening, as we viewed the sculpture and discussed where it should be displayed, Joe asked me, "What does this piece say to you?"

The badly demolished plane, the title, and the salute of the pilot, also a form of "farewell" suggested to me only one thing.

"Oh, I don't know," I said. "But it must mean the aviator has been shot down, was killed, and his salute is his heroic good-bye."

"Yes, it *could* mean that," Joe reluctantly agreed. "But it also could mean something *else*, I think."

"Well, what does it say to you?" I asked.

"I think the aviator is an ace who has survived this kind of crash before and that he also walks away from this one. I think he is saluting the Red Baron. (Remember aviators were a very chivalrous lot during World War I.) I can imagine him saying, 'Okay, buddy, you got me this time, but watch out for me tomorrow.' "

"Interesting," I replied. "I don't think I *ever* would have thought of that." I wanted to ask, "If so, why the title?" but something made me hesitate.

Joe continued, "And then, of course, it also could be that the aviator, realizing what a narrow escape he has had, is in fact saluting God, meaning, 'Thank you, Lord, for sparing my life.' " He was silent for several moments, in deep reflection, and then he added, "Yes, I really think that is what this piece *is* saying. His salute is not skyward but heavenward, and is directed to God."

I thought: "Oh, Nita, you bumbling idiot! Why couldn't you have said that instead of saying it meant death?" Joe so obviously wanted and needed to believe it meant life—life miraculously prolonged against almost insuperable odds. He needed to believe in miracles, not only for the World War I aviator but more especially for himself. *Why* couldn't I have been more perceptive? Why couldn't I have added the support he needed just then?

Quickly agreeing, I said, "Yes, now that you mention it, of course that is it." Then I said something about Joe having the advantage over me; after all, he and the aviator had been friends for some time and, therefore, he had had the opportunity to formulate a better opinion.

But it wasn't the same assurance that it might have been

had I thought more quickly. As I had done on other occasions when I wished so much to share his burden and muffed my opportunity to do so, I vanished into the solitude of the shower—and cried bitter tears.

The sculpture was displayed in the foyer, where it remains—now somewhat incongruously out of place in a feminine and pastel setting. Nevertheless, that is "his place," and I will not move the aviator. He still is saluting heavenward, to God. And on this anniversary of man's first flight, I salute him in memory of my beloved Joe and all other courageous aviators of the world.

Saturday, December 20

A really strange "coincidence" happened today. I was dusting and picked up my beautiful antique book holder, a gift from a friend, on which had been placed an open family Bible. As I did so, my eyes chanced to fall upon these verses of Scripture:

> O Lord, my heart is not lifted up,
> my eyes are not raised too high;
> I do not occupy myself with things
> too great and too marvelous for me.

> But I have calmed and quieted my soul,
> like a child quieted at its mother's breast;
> like a child that is quieted is my soul.
> (Ps. 131:1-2)

The message is so personal, as though it had been written expressly for me, this Psalm composed so long ago! The first verse describes me as I am (indeed, my heart is not lifted up!); the second as I wish to be. Oh, dear Lord, how marvelous it would be if I could truly say, "like a child that is quieted is my soul."

Coincidence? I think not. Thank you, God, for the beauty and the comfort of the Psalms—for your Word. Help me to hear your message through them—to know, today, tomorrow, and forever that you are God.

Wednesday, December 31

The last day of the year, a time for taking inventory, for appraisal. I can't say I'm very pleased with the way I've spent this past year. I've wasted so much precious time, time that is gone forever—a gift from God. I'm thankful, with the approach of a new year, that I have a second chance—an opportunity to do better, to give a better accounting of the gift of life—of time.

I've now kept this journal a full year. It is time to bring it to a close. One wishes the tapestry might have been woven of more brightly gleaming threads—at least acquiescence, if not radiance. But no, it consists mostly of the somber-hued blacks and grays of loneliness, insecurity, and unresolved grief.

Has writing this journal each day been constructive? I think so. But how far have I progressed, if at all? Am I more secure? Less questioning? Happier? Have I moved even a few rungs up the ladder?

Where do I go from here—into this new year and new chance that are on the horizon? Only time, a day at a time, can provide answers to these and all other questions begging solution, of which there remain many.

For now, lines from Robert Frost's poem, "A Leaf-Treader" sum up the year just ending for me:

> Perhaps I have put forth
> too much strength
> and been too fierce from fear.
> I have safely trodden
> underfoot the leaves
> of another year.

I plead guilty. I *have* exerted too much strength, and been too fierce from fear. But somehow, I *have* gotten through the year. No small accomplishment, that—this first year without my beloved.

Awaiting the ringing out of the old year, and the ringing in of a new, more promising one, I close this unhappy chapter of my life. I seek God's forgiveness for having so frequently rejected not only His gift of time but, worse, for having rejected Him and the healing balm of His love.

In prayer, I claim His promise:

"I will restore to you the years that the locust hath eaten" (Joel 2:25 KJV).

NOTES

NOTES

NOTES

NOTES

NOTES

NOTES